U.S. Fish and Wildlife Service
Region 2
Contaminants Program

CONTAMINANTS INVESTIGATION OF ARANSAS DREDGE SPOIL ISLANDS TEXAS, 1988-1989

---

by

Stephen M. Robertson, Thomas W. Schultz
Lawrence R. Gamble and Thomas C. Maurer

U.S. Fish and Wildlife Service
Fish and Wildlife Enhancement
Corpus Christi Field Office
Campus Box 338, 6300 Ocean Drive
Corpus Christi, Texas 78412

December 1991

CONTAMINANTS INVESTIGATION OF
ARANSAS DREDGE SPOIL ISLANDS, TEXAS,
1988-1989

Study Identifier

R2-88-2- 115

Prepared By

U.S. Fish and Wildlife Service
Ecological Services
Corpus **Christi,** Texas

Authors

Stephen M. Robertson
Thomas W. Schultz
Lawrence R. Gamble
Thomas C. Maurer

Under the Supervision of

Rogelio Perez
Field Supervisor

December 1991

ABSTRACT

Organochlorine, trace element, and petroleum hydrocarbon contaminants were examined in sediments and biota from dredge spoil islands adjacent to Aransas National Wildlife Refuge, Texas. Trace elements were 200-500% higher in spoil sediments than local bays. Mercury levels were not elevated in either sediments or biota; other trace elements were detected at moderate levels in most biota samples. Sheepshead minnows from Aransas dredge spoil sites had higher levels of most trace elements than sheepshead minnows from a control site in Flour Bluff, Texas, whereas trace element levels in water boatmen from Aransas dredge spoil sites were generally lower than water boatmen from an evaporation pond in California.

Organochlorines were not detected in sediments, and the low levels of aliphatic hydrocarbons detected in sediments are assumed to be primarily of biogenic origin. Aromatic hydrocarbons were also detected in sediments and biota, but at very low concentrations. In general, this study indicates that a majority of contaminants evaluated were below levels of concern, however, chromium, copper, and lead were detected at elevated levels in both sediment and biota and should be considered as part of future monitoring programs.

TABLE OF CONTENTS

Page

ABSTRACT   ii

LIST OF TABLES   iv

LIST OF FIGURES   iv

INTRODUCTION   1

METHODS AND MATERIALS   3

    Sediment   3

    Biota   3

    Data Analysis   8

RESULTS AND DISCUSSION   9

    Organochlorines   9

    Trace Elements   9

    Petroleum Hydrocarbons   21

CONCLUSIONS   24

ACKNOWLEDGEMENTS   24

LITERATURE CITED   25

LIST OF TABLES

Table   Page

1. Elements and compounds analyzed in sediment and biota from the
   Aransas Bay dredge spoil, Texas, 1988-89   6

2. Detection limits and analytical methods used in the analysis
   of sediment and biota samples collected from the Aransas Bay
   dredge spoil islands, Texas, 1988-89   7

3. Geometric means and ranges of selected elements in sediments
   from spoil deposits in Aransas Bay, Texas, 1988-89, and
   comparative data from other studies   *10*

4. Geometric means and ranges of selected trace elements
   in sediments from spoil deposits by sample site in Aransas Bay,
   Texas, **1988-89**   13

5. Arithmetic means and ranges of selected trace elements in biota
   from spoil deposits in Aransas Bay, Texas, 1988-89   14

6. Arithmetic means and ranges of selected elements in sheepshead
   minnows (*Cyprinodon variegatus*) from spoil deposits in Aransas
   Bay, Texas, 1988-89, and comparative data from a control site
   and other studies and other species   17

7. Means and ranges of selected elements in water boatmen from spoil
   deposits in Aransas Bay, Texas, 1988-89, and comparative data
   from other studies   20

8. Arithmetic means and ranges of selected alkanes in sediments (ppm
   wet weight) from spoil deposits by sample site in Aransas Bay,
   Texas, 1988-89   22

LIST OF FIGURES

Figure

1. Location of Aransas Bay, Texas

2. Location of sediment and biota sample sites

iv

INTRODUCTION

The deposition of dredge spoil material from the creation and maintenance of navigation channels along the Texas coast has received a great deal of scrutiny from the U.S. Fish and Wildlife Service (Service) and other resource agencies. Although numerous concerns have been raised regarding this activity (Natural Resource Maintenance Dredging Working Group **1988**), the disposal of contaminated dredge material is of special concern to the Service's Environmental Contaminants program.

Agricultural activities, oil and gas exploration and production, petrochemical refining, ore processing plants, urban runoff, and municipal wastewater discharges are major contributors of contaminants to Texas bay systems. These contaminants include petroleum hydrocarbons, heavy metals, and pesticides. Due to the hydrophobic nature of many of these contaminants, they tend to adsorb to suspended solids and sediments that settle out onto bay bottoms and into existing navigation channels. In many areas, sediment samples have been found to contain alarming levels of contaminants. In response to this problem, material that is dredged from navigation channels is often placed in confined disposal areas, if it is determined to be unacceptable for open water disposal (Palermo 1988).

After dredging has ceased, confined disposal areas can become attractive to a variety of birds, providing vegetated areas and **ponded** water for feeding and nesting. White and Cromartie (1985) observed 56 species of birds feeding in a confined disposal area in **Nueces** Bay, including great blue herons (*Ardea herodias*), snowy egrets (*Egretta thula*), tricolored herons (*Egretta tricolor*), green-winged teal (*Anas crecca*), northern shoveler (*Anas clypeata*), black necked stilts (*Himantopus mexicanus*), American avocet (*Recurvirostra americana*) and willets (*Cafopfrophorus semipalmatus*).

Very little is known about the potential contaminant threats posed to birds that feed in ponds found within confined disposal areas. Heavy metals (cadmium, mercury, lead, selenium, and zinc) were examined by White and Cromartie (1985) in three bird species, comparing those utilizing a confined disposal area to natural control sites. Only selenium was found at higher levels in birds feeding in the confined disposal area. They did not examine these birds for other contaminants such as aromatic hydrocarbons, aliphatic hydrocarbons, or organochlorines.

The primary goal of this study was to gain preliminary information on the potential threat that contaminants in confined disposal areas adjacent to Aransas National Wildlife Refuge (Aransas NWR) pose to birds that utilize these areas, including the endangered whooping crane (*Grus americana*) that often feeds on the dredge spoil study sites. In addition to concerns over potential contaminants in the spoil materials and their effects on natural resources, this study was also prompted by documentation by the Corps of Engineers in 1986 of a sediment sample from within the study area with an unusually high level of mercury

I

(over 2 ppm). This sample was taken from an area which had received fugitive dredge spoil sediments from a breach in the containment dike on Rattlesnake Island. This high mercury level prompted great concern because there was no obvious or expected source to which it could be attributed. This study was intended, in part, to follow up on this concern and determine if greater alarm over local mercury levels was warranted.

METHODS AND MATERIALS

Sediment

Surface soil and sediment samples were collected at 25 sites within five spoil areas adjacent to the Aransas NWR. Five sediment samples were taken at each of the five spoil islands. Samples were collected to ensure representative coverage of the various conditions within each spoil area, such as in both wet and dry, high and low areas, etc. In dry areas, soil was scraped from the top six inches with a stainless steel scoop. An Ekman dredge was used for sampling in wet or submerged areas. The Aransas Bay locality is shown in Figure 1, and Figure 2 shows the locations of the sample sites. Sample jars and lid liners were chemically cleaned with acid and organic solvents according to U.S. Environmental Protection Agency procedures (EPA 1982). Sediment samples were analyzed for trace elements, aromatic hydrocarbons, alkanes, pesticides, and **PCBs** (Table 1). Trace elements were analyzed at **Hazelton** Laboratories of America, Inc. Using inductively coupled plasma emission spectroscopy to determine levels of all of the elements except arsenic, selenium, and mercury. Arsenic and selenium levels were measured by hydride generation with atomic absorption, and cold vapor atomic absorption was used for the mercury analysis. Blanks, duplicates, spiked samples, and standards were used for quality control and quality assurance, and the results monitored by personnel of the Service's Patuxent Analytical Control Facility (Patuxent). Aromatic hydrocarbons, alkanes, pesticides, and **PCBs** were analyzed at the Geochemical and Environmental Research group of Texas A&M University (GERG). Capillary gas chromatography (CGC) with flame ionization was used to determine aliphatic hydrocarbons. Pesticides and **PCBs** were analyzed by CGC with electron capture, and aromatic hydrocarbons were quantified by mass spectrometer in the SIM mode. Blanks, duplicates, spiked samples, and standards were used for quality control and quality assurance, which was monitored by Patuxent. Elements and compounds analyzed in this study are given in Table 1., and the detection limits are shown in Table 2.

Biota

Composite samples of several organisms that utilize the ponds in the confined disposal areas were collected for analysis. Sheepshead minnows, water boatmen, mosquito larvae, fiddler crabs, and tadpoles were collected from among four spoil islands, and sheepshead minnows were also collected from one control site in Corpus Christi, Texas. All biota samples were analyzed for organochlorines, trace elements, and aromatic hydrocarbons.

Analyses of 21 trace elements were performed at the Environmental Trace Substance Research Center in Columbia, Missouri. Trace elements were determined using inductively coupled plasma emission spectroscopy. Hydride generation with atomic absorption was used for arsenic and selenium determination and cold vapor atomic absorption was used for

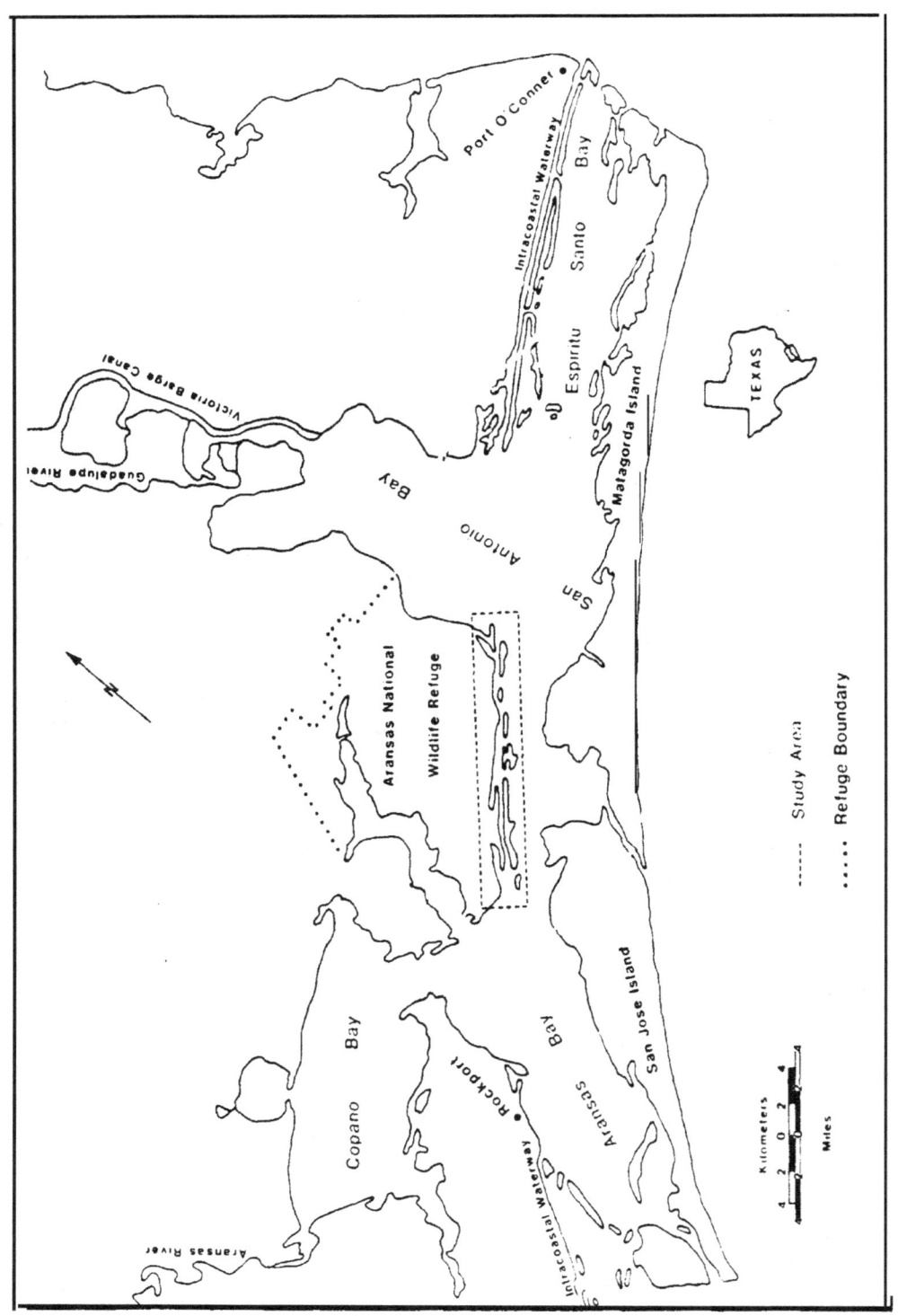

¹Figure 1. **Areas** included in the **study.**

4

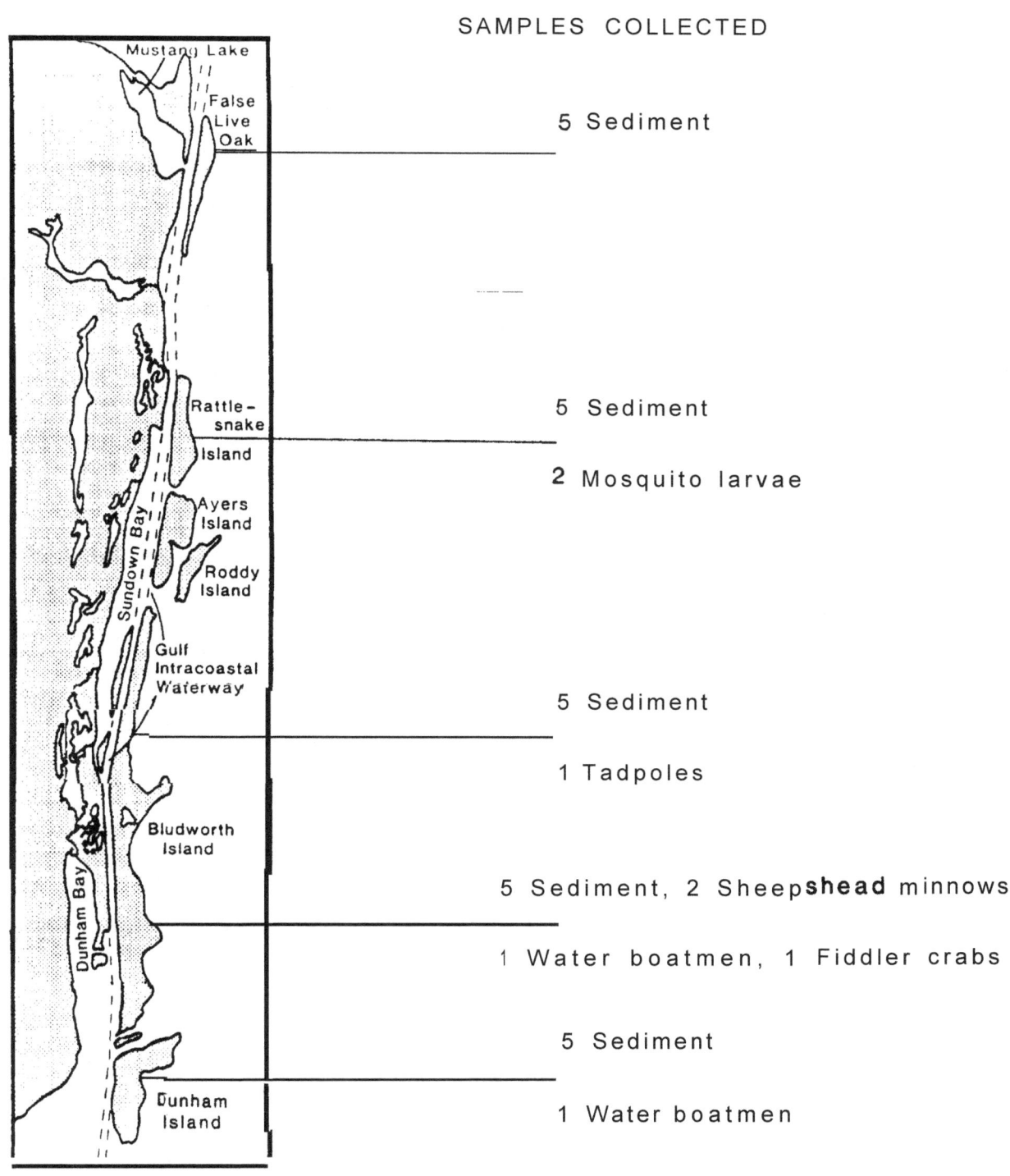

5 Sediment

5 Sediment

2 Mosquito larvae

5 Sediment

1 Tadpoles

5 Sediment, 2 Sheep**shead** minnows

1 Water boatmen, 1 Fiddler crabs

5 Sediment

1 Water boatmen

Figure 2. Locations of sediment and biota sample sites

Table 1. Elements and compounds analyzed in sediment and biota from the Aransas Bay dredge spoil, Texas, 1989.

Elements	Organochlorines	Aromatic Hydrocarbons	Alkanes[1]
Aluminum	alpha-BHC	Naphthalene	N-C12
Antimony'	beta-BHC	2 Methyl Naphthalene	N-C13
Arsenic	delta-BHC	Biphenyl	N-C14
Barium	gamma-BHC[2]	2,6 Dimethyl Naphthalene	N-C15
Beryllium	Total BHC's[2]	Acenaphthene	N-C16
Boron	Aldrin	Methyl Naphthalene	N-C17
Cadmium	hepta epoxide	Flourene	Pristane
Chromium	alpha chlordane	Phenanthrene	N-C18
Copper	gamma chlordane	Anthracene	Phytane
Iron	oxy chlordane	1 Methyl Phenanthrene	N-C19
Lead	trans nonachlor	Fluoranthrene	N-C20
Magnesium	cis nonachlor	Pyrene	
Manganese	Dieldrin	Chrysene	
Mercury	Endrin	Benzo(a)anthracene	
Molybdenum	Mirex	Benzo(b)fluoranthrene	
Nickel	o,p' - DDE	Benzo(k)fluoranthrene	
Selenium	o,p' - DDD	Benzo(a)pyrene	
Silver	o,p' - DDT	Benzo(e)pyrene	
Strontium	PIP' - DDE	Perylene	
Thallium	PIP' - DDD	Indeno pyrene	
Tin'	PIP' - DDT	Dibenzo anthracene	
Vanadium	Total DDT's[1]	Benzo (g,h,i,)perylene	
Zinc	Total PCB's	Acenaphthylene	
	Toxaphene	Methyl Naphthalene	
	Lindane[1]		
	Heptachlor		
	HCB		

[1] Sediments only

[2] Biota only

6

Table 2. Detection limits and analytical methods used in the analysis of **sediment and biota samples collected from the Aransas** Bay dredge spoil islands, Texas, **1988-89.**

ELEMENT	BIOTA PPM (DRY WT)	Method	SEDIMENT PPM (DRY WT)	Method
SE	0.1	HY	0.5	
HG	0.005	CV	0.025	
As	0.2	HY	0.005	
AG	2.0	ICP	5.0	ICPa
AL	0.4	ICPp	10.0	ICPa
BA	0.1	ICP	5.0	ICPa
BE	0.03	ICPp	0.5	ICPa
CD	0.1	ICPp	0.5	ICPa
CR	0.4	ICPp	1.0	ICPa
CU	0.02	ICPp	2.5	ICPa
FE	0.1	ICPp	10.0	ICPa
MG	3.0	ICP	100.0	ICPa
MN	0.2	ICPp	1.5	ICPa
MO	1.0	ICP	5.0	ICPa
NI	0.7	ICPp	4.0	ICPa
PB	0.5	ICPp	10.0	ICPa
SN	NA		5.0	ICPa
SR	0.1	ICI?	1.0	ICPa
TL	0.6	ICPp	0.1	
V	0.3	ICP	5.0	ICPa
ZN	0.1	ICPp	2.0	ICPa

COMPOUND	PPM (WET WEIGHT)	PPM (WET WEIGHT)
ORGANOCHLORINES	0.01	0.05
TOXAPHENE	0.10	0.50
PCB's	0.01	0.05
TOTAL PCB's	0.1	0.5
POLYCYCLIC AROMATIC HYDROCARBONS	0.01	0.01

NA   Not Analyzed
ICP   . **Inductively coupled plasma**
ICPa   Inductively coupled plasma with acid extraction
ICPp   **Inductively** coupled plasm with **preconcentration**
HY   **Hydride** generation **atomic apsorption**
cv   Cold vapor **atomic** absorption

mercury. **Preconcentration** methods were used to enhance detection limits for aluminum, beryllium, cadmium, chromium, copper, iron, manganese, nickel, lead, thallium, and zinc.

Analyses of organic compounds were performed at the GERG. Aromatic hydrocarbons, alkanes, and organochlorines were determined using gas chromatography with mass spectrophotometry for confirmation. Patuxent monitored quality control at these laboratories. Nominal detection limits for the chemicals and elements analyzed in biota are given in Table 2.

Data Analysis

Minimum and maximum values were determined for all organochlorine, trace element, and petroleum hydrocarbon concentrations found above detection limits. Geometric means were determined in those instances where more than 50% of the samples were above detection limits. In those cases where geometric means were calculated, one-half the detection limit was used for those samples below detection limits. The numerical log of each value was taken and then the mean of the logs was calculated. The antilog of the mean was then taken to convert the value back to the arithmetic scale. Arithmetic means were calculated when the number of samples was low (n=2). All trace elements and petroleum hydrocarbons are presented in parts per million (ppm) or the equivalent micrograms per gram (ug/g).

RESULTS AND DISCUSSION

ORGANOCHLORINES

Neither **PCBs** nor organochlorine pesticides were found above the detection limits in sediment and biota samples of this study. The National Academy of Sciences and National Academy of Engineers (1972) established a level of 1 ppm of total DDT in biota as the recommended level for protection of aquatic life. Samples in this study had concentrations less than 0.05 ppm.

TRACE ELEMENTS

Sediments

Twenty-one of 23 trace elements were found above detection limits in sediment. Molybdenum and silver were the only elements not found above detection limits, although tin was found in only one sediment sample. The geometric mean and ranges of selected trace elements in sediment are presented in Table 3. These values are compared both to results from a previous study (Gamble et al. 1989) on the overall bay system, and to geochemical baselines for minor elements in soils in the western United States (Shacklett and Boernaen 1984). All trace element in sediment data from this study are presented in parts per million (ppm) dry weight.

Arsenic
Arsenic was detected in all sediment samples. The geometric mean (GM) was 3.98 ppm (dry weight), with a minimum of 0.59 ppm and maximum of 7.46 ppm. These values are elevated as compared to the overall bay system mean of 1.8 ppm (Gamble et al. 1989), but are below levels of concern expressed by Eisler (1988).

Cadmium
Cadmium was not found above detection limits in any of the sediment samples from the study area. This is consistent with results reported from the surrounding bay system, where only 3% of the sediment samples were above detection limits for this element (Gamble et al. 1989). In contrast, much higher levels (up to 19.9 ppm wet weight) were detected by White and Cromartie (1985) in Corpus Christi Bay dredge spoil sediments.

Chromium
Chromium was detected in all sediment samples, and ranged between 2.06 and 33.8 ppm, with a GM of 14.57 ppm. Some levels were elevated relative to values reported for the the GM of 5.9 in the local bay system (Gamble et al. 1989), warranting some concern. The source of elevated levels of chromium is likely from oil and gas production activities and

Table 3. Geometric means and ranges (in parentheses) of selected elements in sediments (ppm dry weight) from spoil deposits in Aransas Bay, Texas, 1988-89, and comparative data frcanother studies.

Element	Aransas Bay Dredge Spoil (n=25)	Local Bays'[1]	corpus Christi Bay Spoil[2] (n=3, wetweight)	Soil Baselines for Western U.S.[3]
As	3.98 (0.589-7.46) 25[4]	1.8 (0.5-5.0)		5.5 (1.2-22)
B	25.46 (2.26-186) 23			23 (5.8-91)
CD	BDL[5]	_[6] (0.3-0.5)	(2.E9.9)	
CR	14.57 (2.06-33.8) 25	5.9 (2.0-20.0)		41 (8.5-200)
CU	15.9 (5.63-26.2) 25	3.2 (0.4-22.0)		21 (4.9-90)
PB	23.96 (5.1-66.2) 19	5.1 (4.0-19.0)	49.2 (37.5-58.3)	(5.5755)
HG	(0.03-0.05) 4	(0.05-0.50)	0.5 (0.4-0.7)	0.046 (0.009-0.25)
NI	9.7 (2.05-20.5) 20	4.8 (1.0-15.0)		15 (3.4-66)
SE	BDL	(0.2-5.1)	2.3 (1.1-8.4)	0.23 (0.04-1.4)
ZN	35.86 (3.7-83.2) 25	16.7 (0.2-79.2)	847.6 (330.3-2343.9)	55 (17-180)

[1] Data from Gamble et. al., 1989

[2] Data from White and Cromartie, 1985

[3] Geometric means and expected 95% ranges from Wells et. al., 1988

[4] Number of samples above detection limit

[5] Belmdetectionlimit

[6] Fewer than 1/2 n above detection limits

heavy shipping traffic in the Gulf Intracoastal Waterway (GIWW), where the maintenance dredging sediments originated.

Copper
Copper was detected in all sediment samples, with a GM of 14.57 and a range of 5.63-26.2 ppm dry weight. These levels were markedly elevated relative to samples collected from the surrounding bays (GM = 3.2 ppm, Gamble et al. **1989**), probably reflecting anthropogenic sources of contamination from shipping-related activity on the GIWW.

Lead
Lead was detected in 19 of 25 sediment samples. The GM of 23.96 ppm indicates elevated levels relative to a GM of 5.1 ppm from the surrounding bay system (Gamble et al. **1989**), but lower than Corpus Christi Bay dredge spoil sites (GM = 49.2 ppm wet weight, White and Cromartie 1985). Harrison (1987) determined that 13 ppm of lead is the background level for soils in the vicinity of Corpus Christi, Texas.

Mercury
This element was detected in only two of 25 sediment samples, with a range of 0.02-0.05 ppm. These levels can be considered characteristic background levels in uncontaminated sediments (Eisler **1987**), and little concern is warranted over mercury concentrations in surface sediments of these dredge spoil disposal areas. The high levels noted by the COE (1986) in fugitive sediments from dredge spoils in the vicinity may have been from a deeper sediment layer. Deeper core sampling of these spoils may be required to resolve this issue. In contrast to the low levels detected by this study, somewhat higher levels averaging 0.5 ppm wet weight were found by White and Cromartie (1985) in dredged sediments of the Corpus Christi, Texas area.

Nickel
Nickel concentrations in sediment were detected in 80% of the sediment samples, with a GM of 9.7 and a range of 2.05-20.5. Although these values are slightly elevated relative to the surrounding area, they are still within acceptable limits.

Selenium
Selenium was not detected in any of the sediment samples in this study. In the Aransas Bay complex (Gamble et al. **1989**), selenium was detected in 25% of sediment samples, and levels up to 8.4 ppm wet weight were detected in dredge spoil in the Corpus Christi, Texas area (White and Cromartie 1985).

Zinc
Zinc levels in sediment ranged from 3.7 to 83.2 ppm, with a GM of 35.86. This value is higher than surrounding areas (Gamble et al. **1989**), but far lower than that from dredge

sediments measured in Corpus **Christi** Bay; 847.6 ppm wet weight (White and Cromartie 1985).

Comparison Between Spoil Islands

The relative load of trace elements was compared by dividing analyses into groups by spoil island (Table 4). North Bludworth spoil island consistently had the highest levels of selected trace elements, approaching double the overall average. Either the high mercury level previously detected in a sample of fugitive sediment from Rattlesnake Island was anomalous, because sediment samples from that site consistently had the lowest levels of selected trace elements, or the source of the higher levels of mercury was from deeper layers of sediment that were not sampled in this study.

Biota

At the dredge spoil sites sampled for this study, macrofaunal diversity and density was limited, narrowing the options for biota sampling. Sheepshead minnows, water boatmen, mosquito larvae, tadpoles, and fiddler crabs were collected from among the sites.

In biota samples, all but two (silver and thallium) of 19 elements were found above detection limits, although molybdenum was found only in mosquito larvae. The arithmetic means and ranges of selected trace elements in biota are given in Table 5. All elemental tissue concentrations are expressed as parts per million (ppm) dry weight.

Arsenic

Arsenic was detected in all biota samples, ranging from 0.85 ppm dry weight in water boatmen from Dunham disposal island to 3.1 ppm in water boatmen from South Bludworth. Arsenic is a trace element that often receives special interest because of its ability, at elevated levels, to produce mutagenic, teratogenic, and carcinogenic effects in mammals (Nagymajtenyi et al. 1985). Although concentrations in most organisms are typically less than 1 ppm, marine organisms are an exception (Eisler 1988a). Arsenic levels in sheepshead minnows from Aransas bay dredge spoil areas were measured at 1.45 ppm, greater than the National Contaminants Biomonitoring Plan (NCBP) 85th percentile of 1.35 ppm' for a variety of freshwater fish from across the U.S. (Schmitt and Brumbaugh 1990). Marine biota have the ability to accumulate arsenic from seawater and food and typically have higher concentrations than freshwater organisms (**Maher** 1985). These higher concentrations are generally not considered harmful to either the organism or to human consumers, because

---

[1] For this and further references to NCBP means and 85th percentiles, original wet weight data has been converted to approximate dry weight basis by multiplying by a factor of five.

Table 4. Gecanetric **means and ranges of selected elements in sediments (ppm dry** weight) **from spoil** deposits by **sample** site in Aransas Bay, 'Texas, 1988-89.

Spoil Island

Element	Dunham (n=5)	South Bludworth (n=5)	North Bludworth (n=5)	Rattlesnake (n=5)	False Live Oak (n=5)
As	5.52 (3.9-6.6)	3.31 (0.6-7.4)	**6.58 (5.1-7.5)**	1.58 (0.9-5.0)	5.28 (4.0-6.3)
B	12.26 **(2.3[1]-40.3)**	30.30 (6.2-61.9)	70.82 (42.9-186.0)	11.53 (6.4-33.3)	35.31 (29.7-43.0)
CD	BDL[2]	BDL	BDL	BDL	BDL
CR	17.51 (13.7-23.6)	14.07 (2.4-33.8)	27.97 (20.4-33.8)	4.88 (2.1-21.4)	19.49 (13.9-24.7)
CU	19.21 (15.4-24.3)	15.80 (5.6-25.4)	23.42 (20.8-26.2)	10.43 (7.0-21.7)	13.65 (12.4-16.9)
PB	18.88 **(6.3[1]-34.0)**	24.80 **(5.1[1]-66.2)**	52.00 (39.0-63.7)	_[3] **(6.0[1]-37.8)**	34.54 (23.6-43.6)
HG	BDL	BDL	_[3] (0.05)	BDL	_[3] (0.03)
NI	**12.46** (8.4-18.5)	9.16 **(2.1[1]-19.7)**	17.72 (X.5-20.5)	_[3] **(2.4[1]-13.5)**	11.48 (9.3-13.7)
SE	BDL	BDL	BDL	BDL	BDL
ZN	52.77 (35.4-83.2)	31.57 (4.1-78.2)	67.94 (54.5-82.4)	11.36 (3.7-53.3)	46.14 (34.6-54.7)

[1] Below detection limit. Value of **1/2** detection limit assigned
[2] **All values** belowdetectionlimit
[3] Fewer than **1/2** values above detection limit

Table 5. **Arithmetic means and ranges of selected elements** inbiota **(ppm dry** weight) **from spoil** sites in **Aransas Bay, Texas, 1988-89.**

E l - t	Rattlesnake I. Mosquitoe Larvae (n=2) [1]	Dunham& So. Bludworth Water Boatmen (n=2)	So. Bludworth Fiddler Crabs (n=1)	No. Bludworth Tadpoles (n=1)	So. Bludworth Sheepshead Minnows (n=2)
As	**1.85** [2] **(1.8-1.9)** [3]	1.98 (0.85-3.1)	2.3	2.6	1.45 (1.4-1.5)
B	**10 (10)**	32.5 (23-42)	6'	37	13.5 (13-14)
CD	0.31 (0.3-0.32)	0.25 (0.2-0.3)	1.50	0.69	**0. 1 (0. 1)**
CR	5.25 (5.2-5.3)	2.85 (2.5-3.2)	1.5	20.0	**2.0 (1.7-2.3)**
CU	15.5 (15.0-16.0)	7.94 **(7.79-8.08)**	125.0	11.1	5.27 (4.90-5.63)
PB	2.75 (2.7-2.8)	1.35 (0.8-1.9)	1.0	8.0	**0.8 (0.6-1.0)**
HG	0.135 (0.13-0.14)	0.10 (0.06-0.13)	0.04	0.04	0.20 (0.19-0.22)
NI	3.45 (3.4-3.5)	2.15 (2.0-2.3)	1.0	10.0	1.0 **(1)**
SE	1.25 (1.2-1.3)	1.25 (0.6-1.9)	2.0	1.7	**2.4 (2.2-2.6)**
ZN	83.3 (82.1-84.5)	76.1 (54.2-98.0)	119.0	58.2	125 (122-127)
% H_2O	87.8 (87.7-87.9)	77.6 (72.6-82.5)	66.4	87.5	70.2 (69.5-70.8)

[1] Number of composite samples

[2] Arithmetic mean

[3] Range

the major form of arsenic in marine organisms (arsenobetaine) is considered relatively harmless (Kaise et al. 1985).

Cadmium

All biota samples analyzed for this study had detectable levels of cadmium, ranging from 0.1 ppm in sheepshead minnows to 1.5 ppm in fiddler crabs, both from South Bludworth. Cadmium levels in sheepshead minnows were below the NCBP 85th percentile of 0.25 ppm (converted from wet weight, Schmitt and Brumbaugh 1990).

Cadmium, generally considered a nonessential trace element (Eisler 1985a), is potentially toxic to most fish and wildlife, particularly freshwater organisms. Marine biota typically contain much higher concentrations than freshwater organisms due to the higher levels of cadmium in seawater (Eisler 1985a).

Eisler (1971) determined in a laboratory study with the mummichog (*Fundulus heteroclitus*), an estuarine fish, that whole body fresh weight concentrations exceeding 5.0 ppm were potentially lethal. In general, concentrations exceeding 2.0 ppm whole body, fresh weight, for vertebrate animals is considered evidence of probable cadmium contamination (Eisler 1985a). The concentrations of cadmium in all sheepshead minnow and tadpole samples from this study (approximately 0.03 and 0.09 ppm respectively, wet weight) were well below these levels.

Eisler (1985a) noted that cadmium tends to biomagnify through trophic levels. The data from this study agrees with this determination. The concentrations in fiddler crabs were slightly higher than those in tadpoles, which in turn were higher than mosquito larvae. Eisler (1985a) determined that wildlife dietary intake exceeding 0.10 ppm cadmium (fresh weight) on a sustained basis should be viewed with caution. Phillips and Russo (1978) warned that oysters are capable of accumulating extremely high levels of cadmium in edible portions, and thus represent a potential hazard to human consumers. The elevated levels of cadmium could have implications for whooping cranes, which at times feed heavily on a variety of invertebrates. Currently whooping cranes often feed in the immediate vicinity of the sample sites.

The source of cadmium detected in this study has not been determined. Anthropogenic sources of cadmium include fertilizers, municipal wastewater, smelter dust and the products of cadmium-bearing materials in fossil fuels. Cadmium was seldom detected above detection limits in sediment (0.5 ppm) but a lower detection limit might have revealed some difference between sites.

Chromium

Chromium was found above detection in all biota samples. Values ranged from 1.7 ppm in sheepshead minnows from South Bludworth to 20 ppm in tadpoles from North Bludworth. Chromium is known to have both lethal and sublethal effects on fish and wildlife, and current evidence suggests that tissue levels in fish and wildlife in excess of 4.0 ppm dry weight are indicative of chromium contamination (Eisler 1986). Both mosquito larvae from Rattlesnake Island (5.25 ppm) and tadpoles from North Bludworth (20 ppm) had concentrations that exceeded this level.

Copper

Copper was detected in all biota samples, from a low of 4.9 ppm in sheepshead minnows from South Bludsworth to a high of 125 ppm in fiddler crabs. Although copper is an essential element for both plants and animals, in sufficient concentration it may also be toxic to a variety of fish and wildlife (EPA 1980). Breteler (1984) placed copper as one of the major threats to ecosystem health relative to other heavy metals.

The concentrations of copper in sea catfish from this area were generally low (GM = 0.06 ppm wet weight: approximately 0.3 ppm DW). Sea catfish collected in the Lower **Laguna** Madre and South Bay, Texas (Gamble et al. **1988),** contained GM levels of 0.36 ppm wet weight (approximately 1.8 ppm dry weight). Copper levels for sheepshead minnows in the current study were considerably higher **(GM=5.27** dry weight). Custer et al. (1986) in a study at Narragansett Bay, Rhode Island, found that killifish (*Fundulus* sp.) from areas of high contamination contained copper levels of 19.2 ppm dry weight, whereas killifish from areas of "less contamination" contained 9.1 ppm. The NCBP geometric mean during 1984 for a variety of fish species nationwide was recently reported as 0.65 ppm wet weight, or approximately 3.25 ppm dry weight (Schmitt and Brumbaugh 1990). Based on these data, it would appear that copper levels in fish samples collected for this study (arithmetic mean of 5.27 ppm dry weight) are within acceptable limits. In addition, when compared to data from samples from other sites (Table 6), copper levels in samples from dredge spoil sites are only slightly higher than a control sample collected for this study, and are considerably lower than values given for the same species on three National Wildlife Refuges in the region (Table 6). Tadpoles and the invertebrates, however, contained much higher concentrations of copper than the sheepshead minnows, indicating a potential threat to higher order consumers, such as wading birds.

Lead

Lead was found above detection limits in all biota samples, ranging from a low of 0.6 ppm in sheepshead minnows to a high of 8 ppm in tadpoles. Lead, both a nonessential and nonbeneficial element, is toxic in most of its chemical forms and can bioaccumulate, causing sublethal effects to hematopoietic, vascular, nervous, renal and reproductive systems (Eisler 1988b). Despite its toxicity, few threshold levels have been established for lead in the tissues of aquatic organisms.

Table 6. Arithmetic means and range (in parentheses) of selected elements in ppm dry weight) in sheepshead minnows (Cyprinidon variegatus) from spoil deposits in Aransas my, Texas, 1988-89, and comparative data from a control site and other studies.

Element	Dredge spoil sites (n=2)[5]	Control Site Corpus Christi (n=1)	Burgentine Lake Aransas NWR[1,2] (n=1)	Resaca de loscuates, Laguna Atascosa NWR[3] (n=1)	Willow Lake, Santa Ana NWR[4] (n=1)
As	1.45[6] (1.4-1.5)	0.4	6.0	CO.21	3.9
B	13.5 (13-14)	3	9.5	<25.0	7.6
CD	0. 1 (0. 1)	0.2	0.15	Cl.00	0.01
CR	2.0 (1.7-2.3)	0.9	2.5	4.70	2.5
cu	5.27 (4.9-5.63)	3.67	24.5	15.00	16.7
PB	0.8 (0.6-1.0)	3.5	1.5	<1.00	1.3
HG	0.20 (0.19-0.22)	0.01	0.35	CO.225	0.14
NI	1 (1)	BDL[7]	10.0	----	0.90
SE	2.4 (2.2-2.6)	0.5	2.0	1.50	0.73
ZN	125 (122-127)	74.3	155	75	59.2

---

[1] Data from Maurer et al. 1989

[2] To facilitate comparisons, originalwetweightdatawas convert&to approximate dry weight basis by multiplying by a factor of 5

[3] Data from Wells et al. 1988

[4] Data from Gamble et al. 1988

[5] Number of composite samples

[6] Arithmetic mean

[7] Eklowdetectionlimit

The concentration of lead in sheepshead minnows (mean 0.8 ppm) was moderately above the NCBP mean of 0.55 ppm (adjusted to DW from Schmitt and Brumbaugh 1990). These lead levels were higher than found in sea catfish in the Lower Laguna Madre and South Bay (Gamble et al. 1988), where the geometric mean was 0.09 ppm. Killifish collected by Custer et al. (1986) from areas of known heavy metal contamination in Narragansett Bay, Rhode Island, contained lead levels of about 10.1 ppm dry weight, and killifish from "less contaminated" areas had levels of about 3.1 ppm. Lead levels in biota from these spoil areas should be considered for future monitoring as part of the Service's Biomonitoring of Environmental Status and Trends (BEST) program.

Mercury
The concentration of mercury-in biota samples was highest in sheepshead minnows from South Bludworth (0.22 ppm). Lowest values were found in fiddler crabs from South Bludworth and tadpoles from North Bludworth, both at 0.04 ppm. Mercury concentrations in biota are of special concern because mercury can bioconcentrate in organisms and biomagnify through the food chain, impacting fish, wildlife, and humans (Eisler 1987b). Although mercury does occur naturally, it has no known biological function. Schmitt and Brumbaugh (1990) recently reported the NCBP mean for mercury in freshwater fish as 0.1 ppm wet weight (about 0.50 ppm dry weight). Mercury concentrations below 0.5 ppm wet weight (about 2.5 ppm dry weight) in tissues are generally accepted as levels typical of unpolluted environments (Abernathy and Cumbie 1977); all biota samples collected from Aransas Bay dredge spoils were below this level, indicating that mercury contamination is not a major concern in the surface sediments and biota of these dredge spoil sites.

Nickel
Nickel was detected in all biota samples, ranging from 1 ppm in fiddler crabs and sheepshead minnows from South Bludworth up to 10 ppm in tadpoles from North Bludworth. Apparently because of its low toxicity to humans, there is a lack of residue data on nickel for comparisons. In addition, nickel does not accumulate in aquatic organisms (Phillips and Russo 1978).

The Panel on Nickel (1975) considered nickel levels below 0.75 ppm wet weight (about 3.75 ppm dry weight) to be normal for aquatic organisms. Except for tadpoles, all biota samples were below this level.

Selenium
Although selenium is an essential trace element, impacts to animals may result from both selenium deficiency and selenium poisoning (Eisler 1985b). Potential effects of high levels of selenium range from physical malformations during embryonic development to sterility and death (Lemly and Smith 1987).

Residue levels of seleium in all biota samples collected during this study were below levels considered to be harmful. Baumann and May (1984) considered that selenium levels of 10 ppm dry weight (adjusted from wet weight) or more in fish tissue may cause toxic effects. All concentrations in sheepshead minnows collected during this study were below this level (maximum of 2.6 ppm), and only slightly above NCBP mean of 2.1 ppm (converted from wet weight, Schmitt and Brumbaugh 1990). Selenium concentrations in water boatmen (1.25 ppm, Table 7) were far below those from water boatmen from a selenium-rich area in California (38 ppm).

Zinc

Zinc is another essential micronutrient that in sufficient concentrations can result in lethal or sublethal effects. Marine fish and oysters have been noted to accumulate higher levels than freshwater organisms (Phillips and Russo 1978, Duke 1967).

The levels of zinc appear elevated in sheepshead minnows (mean=125 ppm) when compared with zinc concentrations detected in fish from other studies. The NCBP mean (Schmitt and Brumbaugh 1990) for zinc in a variety of fish species is 108.5 ppm (approximated from wet weight). Gamble et al. (1989) found sea catfish in the Aransas Bay complex had a geometric mean of 735 ppm (approximated from wet weight). Custer et al. (1986) detected 202 ppm dry weight zinc in killifish from a site considered highly contaminated with heavy metals in Narragansett Bay, Rhode Island. Although the zinc levels appear slightly elevated, the biological significance of these levels is not known. These concentrations are well below the level of 1,000 ppm wet weight zinc used by Australia as a standard for sea foods (Talbot and Creagh, 1985). Zinc levels in biota from spoil areas should be considered for future monitoring as a part of Aransas **NWR's** portion of BEST.

Comparison between spoil sites

Biota comparisons between dredge spoil sites investigated in this study are hampered by the limited biota available for collections. Water boatmen were collected from two of the study sites, Dunham and South Bludworth spoil islands (Table 7). Trace element levels in water boatmen did not uniformly conform with geometric means of sediment trace elements from their respective collection sites (Tables 4 and 7). However, this is not unexpected because the range measured for trace elements was broad and overlapping for these particular spoil islands.

Table 7.   **Means and** ranges of selected elements **(ppm** dry weight) in water boatmen **from spoil deposits in Aransas** Bay, Texas, 1988-89, **and comparative data from other studies.**

Aransas Bay **Dredge Spoil** Sites

Element	South Bludworth (n=1)	Dunham (n=1)	Westfarmers evaporationponds, CA[1] (n=11)
As	3.1	0.85	0.6[2] (0.3-3.0)[3]
B	23	42	200 (150-570)
CD	0.2	0.3	2.5 (2.3-11)
CR	3.2	2.5	3.6 (2.3-20)
CU	8.08	7.79	49.0 (45-170)
PB	1.9	0.8	----
HG	0.13	0.06	co.4 (<0.4)
NI	2.0	2.3	4.6 (2.2-21)
SE	1.9	0.6	38 (33-140)
ZN	98	54.2	59 (55-120)
%H$_2$O	82.5	72.6	

[1] **Data from** Schroeder et al. 1988

[2] **Data represent the lowest geometric mean concentration in water boatmen from an individual pond**

[3] Range of values measured in 11 water boatmen samples from several ponds

PETROLEUM HYDROCARBONS

Sediment

All eleven of the selected aliphatic hydrocarbons (alkanes) were found above detection limits in at least one sediment sample (Table 8). However, only pristane was detected in over 50% of the samples. Nearly all alkanes were detected at relatively low levels, in the range of 0.01-0.1 ppm wet weight, with no samples exceeding 0.5 ppm.

Aliphatic hydrocarbons are a major component of petroleum products (Sandmeyer 1981, National Academy of Sciences 1985). Armstrong et al. (1979) listed several alkanes found in crude oil at separator platforms in Trinity Bay, Texas, including several of the selected alkanes investigated in this study. These selected alkanes are also components of kerosene, jet and turbo fuels, and lubricating oils (Sandmeyer 1981).

Several alkanes (the odd-numbered carbon n-alkanes) -are also produced by algae and phytoplankton (Blumer et al. 1971, Coates et al. 1986). In particular, n-pentadecane, n-heptadecane, n-nonadecane, and pristane have been noted as alkanes produced by marine algae (Shaw et al. 1986). Pristane is also a component of calanoid copepods and may be detected in fish that have fed on these copepods (Blumer et al. 1963, Blumer 1967).

A determination of the contribution from petroleum and biogenic sources is possible only on a relative basis. A predominance of odd-numbered carbon n-alkanes would suggest a biogenic source (Sanders et al. 1980, National Academy of Sciences 1985). In petroleum hydrocarbons, there is no preponderance of odd or even-numbered carbon n-alkanes, and the occurrence of phytane suggests a petroleum hydrocarbon source (National Academy of Science, 1985). The alkane most frequently detected (pristane) is usually associated with biogenic sources. Phytane was detected in nine sediment samples, however, always at lower concentrations than pristane, so it appears that the majority of alkanes detected in this study were of biogenic origin.

Sediment samples from the dredge spoil study sites were analyzed for 24 polycyclic aromatic hydrocarbons (PAHs); of these, 15 were detected in at least one of 25 samples. Only six aromatics (l-methyl phenanthrene, perylene, fluoranthrene, pyrene, benzo (a) anthracene, and chrysene) were detected in over 50% of the samples. Although the last four were detected in all samples, no levels above 0.03 ppm wet weight were detected for any PAH in any sample.

A variety of petroleum products are transported along the Gulf Intracoastal Waterway, from which the spoil examined in this study originates. Because oil spillage is considered the major source of PAHs in aquatic environments, these are the most likely sources of the

Table 8. Arithmetic means and ranges of selected alkanes in sediments (ppm wet weight) from spoil deposits by sample site in Aransas Bay, Texas, 1988-89.

Alkane	Dunham (n=5)	south Bludworth (n=5)	North Bludworth (n=5)	Rattlesnake (n=5)	False Live Oak (n=5)
N-C12 (Dodecane)	BDL[1]	BDL	BDL	BDL	---[2] (0.21)
N-C13 (Tridecane)	BDL	BDL	B D L	--- (0.3)	--- (0.08-0.47)
N-C14 (Tetradecane)	BDL	BDL	BDL	---	---
N-C15 (Pentadecane)	BDL	BDL	BDL	(0.13)	--- (0.05-0.26)
N-cl6 (Hexadecane)	BDL	BDL	BDL	--- (0.02)	--- (0.01-0.11)
N-C17 (Heptadecane)	BDL	BDL	--- (0.01)	BDL	--- (0.02)
Pristane	--- (0.01)	BDL	0.185[3] (0.11-0.45)	0.096 (0.04-0.25)	0.044 (0.02-0.06)
N-cl8 (Octadecane)	BDL	BDL	BDL	BDL	-- (0.01)
Phytane	BDL	BDL	--- (0.01-0.03)	--- (0.02-0.05)	0.02 (0.01-0.03)
N-C19 (Nonadecane)	BDL	BDL	0.029[3] (0.01-0.09)	--- (0.01)	0.026[3] (0.01-0.08)
N-C20 (Eicosane)	BDL	BDL	0.042 (0.02-0.1)	--- (0.02)	0.035[3] (0.01-0.1)

[1] All values below detection limit

[2] Fewer than 50% of values above detection limit

[3] Value of 1/2 detection limit assigned to any value below detection limit

PAHs detected in this study.

<u>Biota</u>

Biota, except for the sheepshead minnows, were analyzed for selected aromatic hydrocarbons (Table 1). Only one (acenaphthylene) of the 24 aromatic hydrocarbons was found even approaching 95% confidence interval detection limits. Levels of acenaphthylene (and all other **PAHs**) were below 0.01 ppm wet weight in all biota samples.

A large information base is developing for **PAHs.** This is primarily due to their toxicity, and several are among the most potent carcinogens known to exist (Eisler 1987a). Like the aliphatic hydrocarbons, **PAHs** may also be biogenically produced by microorganisms, algae, and macrophytes. A variety of other sources contribute to **PAHs** in the environment. In aquatic environments, petroleum spillage is the major source of **PAHs** (Eisler 1987a).

Fish have been noted for containing unusually low levels of **PAHs** (Lawrence and Weber 1984, Baumann et al. 1988). This has been attributed to their ability to rapidly metabolize **PAHs** (Neff et al. 1976, Lawrence and Weber 1984, Niimi and Palazzo 1986). Crustaceans also have the enzymes necessary to metabolize **PAHs** (Statham et al. 1976). Bivalves, however, lack the necessary enzymes to metabolize **PAHs,** and therefore tend to accumulate these compounds upon exposure. From the above, it is apparent that PAH contamination does not currently pose a threat to fish and wildlife using the dredge spoil islands sampled in this study.

CONCLUSIONS

Based upon the results of this study, the sediments of the spoil islands evaluated appear to be moderately contaminated with chromium, copper, and lead, most likely due to the dredging and deposition of sediments polluted from anthropogenic sources associated with shipping activity on the adjacent Gulf Intracoastal Waterway and the area's oil and gas production activities. In addition, chromium, copper, and lead were detected in sufficient concentration in amphibians and invertebrates from these spoil islands to pose a potential threat to fish and wildlife (particularly wading birds and shorebirds) that utilize those organisms as a source of food. Despite being undetected in spoil sediments, cadmium was detected in mosquito larvae (5.25 ppm) and tadpoles (20 ppm) from these spoil islands, well in excess of the 4.0 ppm criteria generally considered as the threshold for biological effects in organisms. Such an occurrence is not unusual, given that the detection limit for cadmium in sediments is 0.5 ppm, and organisms can bioconcentrate cadmium approximately 64 times that of their surrounding's ambient levels. Implications of the above conclusions are that monitoring of potentially affected fish and wildlife resources, such as wading birds, shorebirds and their prey items, should be periodically conducted to detect and possibly avoid adverse impacts from the utilization of those dredge spoil islands as feeding habitat.

ACKNOWLEDGEMENTS

We thank the staff of the Aransas National Wildlife Refuge for facilitating field work for this study. This report was reviewed by David Potter, Charlie Chandler, Brian Pridgeon, Charlie Sanchez, and Lori Robertson, whom we thank for helpful and constructive comments.

LITERATURE CITED

Abernathy, A.R. and P.M. Cumbie. 1977. Mercury accumulation by largemouth bass (Micropterus salmoides) in recently impounded reservoirs. Bull. Environ. Contam. Toxicol. 17:595-602.

Armstrong, H.W., K. Fucik, J.W. Anderson, and J.M. Neff. 1979. Effects of oilfield brine effluent on sediment and benthic organisms in Trinity Bay, Texas. Marine Environ. Res. 2:55-68.

Baumann, P.C. and T.W. May 1984. Selenium residues in fish from inland waters of the United States. Workshop proceedings: the effects of trace elements on aquatic ecosystems. Electric Power Research Institute. EPRI EA-3329, Project 1631. 16 pp.

Baumann, P.C., J.L. Zajicek, and C.J. Schmitt. 1988. A better way to determine exposure of fish to polycyclic aromatic hydrocarbons. U.S. Fish Wildl. Serv. Information Bull. No. 88-14.

Blumer, M. 1967. Hydrocarbons in the digestive tract and liver of basking shark. Science. 156:390-391.

Blumer, M., R.R.L. Guillard, and T. Chase. 1971. Hydrocarbons of marine phytoplankton. Marine Bio. 8:183-189.

Blumer, M. and M.M. Mullin. 1963. Pristane in zooplankton. Science. 140:974.

Breteler, R.J. 1984. Chemical Pollution of the Hudson-Raritan Estuary. NOAA Tech. Memo. NOS/OMA 7.

Coates, M., D.W. Connel, J. Bodero, G.J. Miller, and R. Back. 1986. Aliphatic hydrocarbons in Great Barrier Reef organisms and environment. Estuarine, Coastal and Shelf Science. 23:99-1 13.

Corps of Engineers. 1986. Biological assesment for Impacts to threatened and endangered species. Habitat restoration, Aransas National Wildlife Refuge, Rattlesnake Island. US Army Engineer District, Galveston, Texas.

Custer, T.W., J.C. Franson, J.F. Moore, and J.E. Myers. 1986. Reproductive success and heavy metal contamination in Rhode Island common terns. Environ. Pol. 41:33-52.

Duke, T.W. 1967. Possible routes of zinc 65 from an experimental estuarine environment to man. J. Water Pollut. Control Fed. **39:536-542.**

Eisler, R. 1971. Cadmium poisoning in Fundulus heteroclitus (Pisces: Cyprinodontidae) and other marine organisms. J. Fish Res. Board Canada. **28:1225-1234.**

Eisler, R. **1985a.** Cadmium hazards to fish, wildlife, and invertebrates: a synoptic review. U.S. Fish Wildl. Serv. Biol. Rep. 85 (1.2). 46 pp.

Eisler, R. 1985b. Selenium hazards to fish, wildlife, and invertebrates: a synoptic review. U.S. Fish Wildl. Serv. Biol. Rep. 85 (1.5) 57 pp.

Eisler, R. 1986. Chromium hazards to fish, wildlife, and invertebrates: a synoptic review. U.S. Fish Wildl. Serv. Biol. Rep. 85 (1.6). 60 pp.

Eisler, R. 1987a. Polycyclic aromatic hydrocarbon hazards to fish, wildlife, and invertebrates: a synoptic review. U.S. Fish Wildl. Serv. Biol. Rep. 85 (1.11). 81 pp.

Eisler, R. 1987b. Mercury hazards to fish, wildlife, and invertebrates: a synoptic review. U.S. Fish Wildl. Serv. Biol. Rep. 85 (1.10). 90 pp.

Eisler, R. 1988a. Arsenic hazards to fish, wildlife, and invertebrates: a synoptic review. U.S. Fish and Wildl. Serv. Biol. Rep. 85 (1.12). 92 pp.

Eisler, R. 1988b. Lead hazards to fish, wildlife, and invertebrates: a synoptic review. U.S. Fish Wildl. Serv. Biol. Rep. 85 (1.14). 134 pp.

Environmental Protection Agency. 1980. Ambient water quality criteria for copper. Washington, D.C. EPA 44015-80-036.

Environmental Protection Agency. 1982. Handbook for sampling and sample preservation of water and wastewater. EPA -600/4-82-029.

Gamble, L.R., G. Jackson, and T.M. Maurer. 1988. Organochlorine, trace element, and petroleum hydrocarbon contaminants investigation of the Lower Rio Grande Valley, Texas, 1985-86. U.S. Fish Wildl. Serv., Ecological Services, Corpus Christi, TX. Unpublished document.

Gamble, L.R., G. Jackson and T.M. Maurer. 1989. Contaminants investigation of the Aransas Bay complex, Texas, 1985-1986. U.S. Fish and Wildl. Serv., Ecological Services, Corpus Christi, TX. Unpublished document.

Harrison, G. 1987. A survey of the lead distribution in the soil of Corpus Christi, Texas. Texas J. of Sci. 39:16-22.

Kaise, T., S. Watanabe, and K. Itoh. 1985. The acute toxicity of arsenobetaine. Chemosphere. 14:1327-1332.

Lawrence, J.F. and D.F. Weber. 1984. Determination of polycyclic aromatic hydrocarbons in some Canadian commercial fish, shellfish, and meat products by liquid chromatography with confirmation by capillary gas chromatography-mass spectrometry. J. Agric. Food Chain. 32:789-794.

Lemly, A.D. and G.J. Smith. 1987. Aquatic cycling of selenium: implications for fish and wildlife. U.S. Fish Wildl. Serv. Fish. Wildl. Leaflet 12. 10 pp.

Maher, W.A. 1985. The presence of arsenobetaine in marine mammals. Comp. Biochem. Physiol. 80C: 199-201.

Maurer, T.C., L.R. Gamble and G. Jackson. 1989. Contaminants investigation of Burgentine Lake, Aransas National Wildlife Refuge, Texas. U.S. Fish Wildl. Serv., Ecological Services, Corpus Christi, TX. Unpublished document.

Nagymajtenyi, L., A. Selypes, and G. Berencsi. 1985. Chromosomal aberrations and fetotoxic effects of atmospheric arsenic exposure in mice. J. Appl. Toxicol. 5:61-63.

National Academy of Sciences. 1985. Oil in the sea: inputs, fates and effects. National Academy Press, Washington, D.C. 601 pp.

National Academy of Sciences, National Academy of Engineers. 1972. Section Ill-freshwater aquatic life and wildlife, water quality criteria. Ecological Research Series. EPA-R3-033.

Natural Resource Agency Maintenance Dredging Working Group. 1988. Issue Paper: Evaluation of the U.S. Army Corps of Engineers' 1975 Environmental Statement on maintenance dredging of the Gulf Intracoastal Waterway, Texas Section. Unpublished document. 35pp.

Neff, J.M., B.A. Cox, D. Dixit, and J.W. Anderson. 1976. Accumulation and release of petroleum-derived aromatic hydrocarbons by four species of marine animals. Mar. Bio. 38:279-289.

Niimi, A.J. and V. Palazzo. 1986. Biological half-lives of eight polycyclic aromatic hydrocarbons (PAHs) in rainbow trout (Salmo gairdneri). Wat. Res. **20:503-507.**

Palermo, M. R. 1988. Field evaluations of the quality of effluent from confined dredged material disposal areas. Tech. Report D-88-l. U.S. Army Corps of Engineers Waterway Experiment Station, Vicksburg, Ms. **62pp.**

Panel on Nickel. 1975. Nickel. Committee on Medical and Biological Effects of Environmental Pollutants, National Research Council, National Academy of Sciences. Wash., D.C. 277 pp.

Phillips, G.R. and R.C. Russo. 1978. Metal bioaccumulation in fisheries and aquatic invertebrates: a literature review. Environmental Research Laboratory. Duluth, MN. **EPA-600/3-78-** 103.

Sanders, H.L., J.F. Grassle, G.R. Hampson, L.S. Morse, S. Garner-Price, and C.C. Jones. 1980. Anatomy of an oil spill: long term effects from the grounding of the barge Florida off West Falmouth, Massachusetts. J. Marine Res. **38:265-380.**

Sandmeyer, E.E. 1981. Aliphatic hydrocarbons. pp. 3175-3220. **In** Patty's Industrial Hygiene and Toxicology, Vol. **2B,** Toxicology. G.D. Clayton and F.E. Clayton (eds.). John Wiley and Sons, New York.

Schmitt, C.J. and W.G. Brumbaugh. 1990. National Contaminant Biomonitoring Program: concentrations of arsenic, cadmium, copper, lead, mercury, selenium and zinc in U.S. freshwater fish, 1976-1984. Arch. Environ. **Contam.** Toxicol. **19:731-747.**

Schroeder, R.A., D.U. Palawski and J. P. Skorupa. 1988. Reconnaissance investigation of water quality, bottom sediment, and biota associated with irrigation drainage in the Tulare Lake Bed Area, Southern San Joaquin Valley, California, 1986-87. U.S. Geological Survey, Water- resources Investigations Report 88-4001.

Shacklett, H.T. and J.G. Boernaen. 1984. Element concentrationsin soils and other surficial materials of the conterminous United States: U.S. Geological Survey Proffesional Paper 1270, 105 p.

Shaw, D.G., T.E. Hogan, and D.J. McIntosh. 1986. Hydrocarbons in bivalve mollusks of Port Valdez, Alaska: consequences of five years' permitted discharge. Estuarine, Coastal and Shelf Science. **23:863-872.**

Statham, C.N., M.J. Melancon, Jr., and J.J. Lech. 1976. Bioconcentration of xenobiotics in trout bile: a proposed monitoring aid for some waterborne chemicals. Science 193:680-681.

Talbot, V. and S. Creagh. 1985. The derivation of threshold mean concentrations of copper and zinc in seawater, to protect edible tropical rock oyster, Saccostrea cuccullata, from exceeding the health (food) standards. Australian Dept. of Conserv. and Environ. Bulletin 212.

White, D.H. and E. Cromartie. 1985. Bird use and heavy metal accumulation in waterbirds at dredge disposal impoundments, Corpus Christi, Texas. Bull. Environ. Con. Tox. 34:295-300.